THE MOST ORGANIZED
MAN IN AMERICA'S

Guide to Moving

ANDREW MELLEN

Copyright © 2019 by Andrew Mellen, Inc.

All rights reserved. This book or any portion thereof
may not be reproduced or used in any manner whatsoever
without the express written permission of the publisher
except for the use of brief quotations in a book review.

www.AndrewMellen.com

Contents

Introduction	1
The Ultimate Moving Checklist	3
Tips & Tricks	17
Getting Ready to Pack	21
Working with Professional Movers	32
DIY Packing & Moving	36
Children & Moving	39
Pets & Moving	41
Moving with Disabilities	44
Resources	46

Introduction

THE BAD NEWS

Moving sucks. In fact, it's right up there with death and divorce as one of the most stressful life events a person can go through.

Acknowledging that moving is stressful is the first step in managing the stress.

Feelings of loss also add to the stress around moving, whether it's a forced relocation or not. Most people see the glass half empty when stressed so you may be more focused on what you're losing in your move rather than on what you're gaining. That's a natural response and one that is easily dealt with through a simple mindset shift.

THE GOOD NEWS

A mentor of mine once told me, "inside every disappointment is the seed of an equal or greater opportunity," and that piece of advice has allowed me to walk through some pretty stressful situations.

Whether you want to move or not, you ARE moving. Accepting that rather than fighting it allows for something remarkable to happen. The key is letting go of your old mindset that only sees the disruption, not the opportunity.

Also, with proper planning, you can virtually eliminate the potential for things to go wrong.

So whether you have a new job (or a new lack of job), your family has changed configuration or your living situation has shifted–roommate moved out, a significant other moved in, you found someplace better to live or your landlord wanted you to leave–moving is a big deal with lots of little details to consider.

It's easy to get overwhelmed–luckily, you've got this book as your guide through the whole process.

Refer to the Ultimate Moving Checklist for a quick run-down on what to do and when to do it, and keep on reading for clear, concise tips on how to do it all in the most efficient, organized, and stress-free way possible

YOUR TAKEAWAY

Here's your final takeaway—you can't escape the stress everyone feels when moving AND with this book you'll avoid everything that could possibly add to your stress… so it's almost like moving is a stress-neutral experience with a bonus opportunity folded in. How's that for a mindset shift?

Now let's get started.

The Ultimate Moving Checklist

3 MONTHS BEFORE MOVE

- ☐ Determine how much money you can/want to spend on your move
- ☐ Determine the costs of leaving your home and moving into your new home
- ☐ Research movers and/or relocation vehicles and get quotes
    - ☐ Ask friends for referrals
    - ☐ Search online using these phrases
        - ☐ Truck/trailer rentals
        - ☐ Moving companies
        - ☐ Exclusive use
        - ☐ Shared use
- ☐ Research transportation options for your family and/or pets
- ☐ Determine any additional storage and packing expenses
    - ☐ Temporary storage in your current location
    - ☐ Temporary storage in your destination location
    - ☐ Special handling/shipping for fragile items
    - ☐ Special handling/shipping for musical instruments
    - ☐ Special handling/shipping for fine art + antiques
    - ☐ Special handling/shipping for vehicles
        - ☐ Car(s)
        - ☐ Motorcycle(s)
        - ☐ ATV(s)
        - ☐ Boats(s)
        - ☐ Other
- ☐ Calculate the first month of living expenses in new location
- ☐ Finalize your complete moving budget

2 MONTHS BEFORE MOVE

- ☐ Decide on your moving method
- ☐ Hire the truck/trailer OR mover with the best quote and reputation
- ☐ Create binder/folder for moving records (estimates, receipts, inventory lists, etc.)
- ☐ Check with your insurance company to see if your move is covered under your existing policy and what the terms of coverage are, then compare with additional insurance your mover is offering
- ☐ Begin to organize your belongings Like With Like to determine size + quantity
- ☐ Determine how much packing supplies will be needed
- ☐ Acquire packing materials
    - ☐ From your mover or local store
    - ☐ Online vendor
        - ☐ Boxes
        - ☐ Crates
        - ☐ Tape
        - ☐ Assorted colored 3x5 cards
        - ☐ Bubble wrap
        - ☐ Newsprint/paper padding
        - ☐ Markers
        - ☐ Other
- ☐ Plan how you will arrange furniture in the new place—use a floor plan or sketch
- ☐ Hold a garage sale and sell, donate, or dispose of anything you don't want to include in your move
- ☐ Return borrowed, checked-out and rented items
- ☐ Get things returned to you that you have lent out

- ☐ Create an inventory by photographing or video recording your household items
- ☐ Notify doctors of your move and ask for referrals to doctors where you're moving
- ☐ Get copies of all medical, dental and veterinary records for the entire household
    - ☐ Printed
    - ☐ Digital on a flash drive
    - ☐ Emailed to you
- ☐ Contact your insurance company to transfer medical, property, fire, and auto insurance policies
- ☐ **Moving with Children:** Arrange and schedule for the transfer of school records and register for new schools
- ☐ Make travel arrangements for the move so that you arrive before the movers' scheduled arrival
- ☐ **Moving for Work:** Find out if your employer will provide moving expense benefits. If you are being transferred by your work, review your employer's moving policy.
- ☐ Schedule disconnection/connection of utilities at old and new place
    - ☐ Phone
    - ☐ Internet
    - ☐ Cable
    - ☐ Water
    - ☐ Garbage
    - ☐ Gas
    - ☐ Electric
    - ☐ Other
- ☐ Plan how you will move vehicles, plants, pets and valuables
- ☐ Make any home repairs that you have committed to making
- ☐ Inform your housekeeper, gardener, handyman and any other regular workers about your move. Ask for referrals for someone at your new location

1 MONTH BEFORE MOVE

☐ Confirm the details of your move with your mover

☐ Figure out the kinds of help you'll need at the new location

- ☐ Housekeeper
- ☐ Cook
- ☐ Gardener
- ☐ Babysitter
- ☐ Tutor
- ☐ Dog walker
- ☐ Plumber
- ☐ Electrician
- ☐ Painter
- ☐ Handyperson
- ☐ Other

☐ Follow up on any referrals from workers and/or begin searching for reliable help at your new location

- ☐ Referrals
- ☐ Craigslist
- ☐ Angie's List
- ☐ Task Rabbit
- ☐ Home Advisor
- ☐ Handy
- ☐ Other

☐ Screen and hire any workers to perform tasks at the new location

☐ Reserve storage unit if needed

☐ Create an inventory list of items and box contents, including serial numbers of major items—use this as an opportunity to update your home inventory and share with your insurance company—and to compare with the moving company's list

☐ Create a plan for unpacking the new home

- ☐ Begin packing non-essential items
- ☐ Begin packing out-of-season items
- ☐ Label boxes by room and contents
    - ☐ Write the room the box belongs in
    - ☐ Assign colors using your 3x5 cards for each room and tape that color card to each carton and container
    - ☐ Make a color key for yourself and to share with movers/helpers
- ☐ Obtain an IRS Change of Address form (Form 8822) by calling (800) 829-1040 or visiting http://www.irs.gov.
- ☐ Obtain a Change of Address Form from your local Post Office https://www.usa.gov/post-office
- ☐ Report your change of address to the DMV if you own vehicles https://dmv.ny.gov/address-change/change-address-my-license-registrations
- ☐ Research the Secretary of State or DMV in your new location for your new ID
- ☐ Schedule any appointments you can to update these items for the first week you're in the new town
- ☐ Get new prescriptions from your doctor(s)
- ☐ If you use an online pharmacy, refill prescriptions for 90 days
- ☐ Find a pharmacy in your new town and transfer prescriptions
- ☐ Give a change of address to:
    - ☐ banks
    - ☐ credit card companies
    - ☐ schools
    - ☐ friends
    - ☐ family
    - ☐ insurance companies
    - ☐ doctors
    - ☐ cell phone providers
    - ☐ magazine and newspaper subscriptions
    - ☐ other

- ☐ Separate valuable items to transport yourself—label as DO NOT MOVE
- ☐ Keep a box out for storing pieces, parts and essential tools that you will want to keep with you on move day—label as PARTS / DO NOT MOVE
- ☐ Cancel automated payment plans and local accounts/ memberships if necessary
- ☐ Moving with Car: Take your vehicle(s) in for a tune-up, especially if you are traveling very far
- ☐ Start using up food you have stored so there is less to move

3 WEEKS BEFORE MOVE

☐ Schedule any services to be performed next week at the new location

☐ Figure out who will give them access

☐ Arrange for them to get access

2 WEEKS BEFORE MOVE

☐ Clean any rooms that have been emptied and make sure nothing was left unpacked

☐ Have services at your new location performed, including:

☐ Deep cleaning

☐ Carpet cleaning

☐ Painting

☐ Repairs

☐ Other

☐ Confirm installation of utilities at your new home:

☐ Phone

☐ Internet

☐ Cable

☐ Water

☐ Garbage

☐ Gas

☐ Electric

☐ Alarm Company

☐ Other

☐ Take or get measurements of your spaces to make sure existing and new furniture fits

☐ Doorways

☐ Hallways

☐ Rooms

☐ Stairs and landings

7 DAYS BEFORE MOVE

- ☐ Confirm move date with your mover
- ☐ Confirm closing/move-in dates with real estate agent and storage facilities

4 DAYS BEFORE MOVE

- ☐ Make sure all deliveries such as newspaper and mail have been cancelled and redirected to the new home
- ☐ Throw a going away party for the kids to say goodbye to their friends
- ☐ Clean up after the party and process any feelings the kids are having

3 DAYS BEFORE MOVE

- ☐ Create a list for your movers of things they will need such as phone numbers, the moving address, and maps—print up and tape near front door (or put in your binder)
- ☐ Make lists of everything you need done on MOVING DAY to share with any helpers
- ☐ Print the lists of instructions and tape them up in each room

2 DAYS BEFORE MOVE

- ☐ Pack any last minute items
- ☐ Arrange for payment for movers and tips for each mover
- ☐ Disconnect and disassemble software such as computers and backup important files on a memory drive
- ☐ Gather all keys, alarm codes, and garage openers and prepare them to be given to the real estate agent or new owner

1 DAY BEFORE MOVE

- ☐ Set your alarm for 1 hour earlier than you think you should

MOVING DAY

- ☐ Confirm you have a padlock or plan to buy one from the truck rental
- ☐ Go early to pick up the truck if you rented one
- ☐ Pick up coffee and breakfast on your way home
- ☐ Put together necessary items to have on move-in day such as:
    - ☐ ID
    - ☐ Wallet
    - ☐ Checkbook
    - ☐ Cash
    - ☐ Drinking water
    - ☐ Toothbrush + toothpaste
    - ☐ Soap
    - ☐ Prescription medications + aspirin
    - ☐ Snacks
    - ☐ Paper plates, cups + recyclable utensils
    - ☐ Towels
    - ☐ Bed sheets
    - ☐ Scissors and/or box knife
    - ☐ Tape
    - ☐ Closing documents and/or lease
    - ☐ Important files
    - ☐ Medical records
    - ☐ Pet food (if needed)
- ☐ Remove bedding and take apart beds
- ☐ Take movers/helpers through the house and share instructions with them
- ☐ Empty, clean, and defrost your refrigerator/freezer
- ☐ Read the Bill of Lading and sign it
- ☐ Make sure you have the moving company's contact information

- ☐ Office number
- ☐ Mobile phone for your driver/crew foreman
☐ Hand your list of phone numbers, the moving address, and maps to the mover's foreman

☐ Lock all the windows and doors

☐ Use a padlock to lock up any rented truck

☐ Walk through your now empty space to check for things left behind—look behind doors

☐ Leave your contact info for new residents to forward mail

☐ Take inventory before movers leave, sign bill of lading

☐ Check all appliances to confirm they are off

☐ Turn off the lights and say goodbye

Moving with Children

☐ Continue fun family rituals and create new ones in the new home

☐ Have a positive attitude about the move to set a good example for kids

MOVING INTO YOUR NEW HOME

PREPARING TO MOVE YOUR THINGS INTO THE NEW SPACE

☐ Before you unpack and unload any vehicles, perform an initial inspection of the new space. Note any damages and take photographs as needed

☐ Verify utilities are working—especially power, water, heating, and cooling

☐ Clean the entire house, including kitchen and bathroom, and vacuum as needed (especially where furniture will be going)

☐ Confirm you have toilet paper, soap and towels in place

☐ Lay down and secure any protective floor covering materials for the movers

☐ Tape colored 3x5 cards to each doorway and door to direct movers/helpers where to put things

☐ Assign homes for all major categories of things using the CATEGORIES worksheet

☐ Assign a purpose for all closets using the CLOSETS worksheet and label them

☐ Walk the space with movers/helpers to familiarize them with destinations

UNLOADING THE TRUCK

☐ Place any large furniture pieces, then unwrap them

☐ Assemble beds with bedding

☐ Place boxes/containers in their proper rooms—do not stack them too high

☐ Group boxes by similar contents whenever possible as you bring them in

☐ Offer drinks and snacks, especially if your helpers are volunteers

☐ When the last box is inside, walk the space to confirm that everything is in the right room

☐ Confirm the truck is empty once everything has been unloaded

☐ Sign any paperwork from the movers

- ☐ Pay and tip movers as needed
- ☐ Take a deep breath and smile

UNPACKING YOUR THINGS

- ☐ Begin unpacking, starting with the kitchen, bathroom and other essential spaces
- ☐ Establish a home in each room for broken down packing materials
- ☐ Use a recycling bag for paper packing materials
- ☐ Use a trash bag for any packing materials that can't be recycled/reused
- ☐ Reserve one box for any peanuts or other reusable packing materials
- ☐ Break down each box as you go and stack them for easy removal
- ☐ Inspect each item for damage as you're unpacking and photograph any damage—note the deadline for insurance claims

KITCHEN

- ☐ As you unpack things that will come in contact with food, wash them or put them in the dishwasher to clean them before you put them away

CLOTHES CLOSETS

- ☐ As you unpack things, make sure everything has a hanger that needs a hanger and refold anything that got shifted during the move

FIRST WEEK IN YOUR NEW HOME
- ☐ Replace locks if needed and make copies of the new keys
- ☐ Choose a lock-out solution in case you lose your new keys
- ☐ Locate the circuit breaker
- ☐ Locate shut-off valves and meters for water and electricity
- ☐ Confirm any security system is working and that you have the correct codes
- ☐ Make sure there are fire extinguishers and smoke detectors in the new home
- ☐ Test smoke detectors, replace batteries as needed
- ☐ If you brought a safe, find a good home for it—or arrange for one to be installed
- ☐ Inspect any in-ground sprinkler systems or other systems that could be auto-scheduled
- ☐ Inspect and test your heating and cooling units, insulation, and ducts
- ☐ Make sure you get any moving deposits back
- ☐ Perform any cosmetic repairs that need to be done
- ☐ Recycle all packing materials—drop off peanuts/bubble wrap at local shipping store
- ☐ Confirm that mail is now arriving at your new address
- ☐ Make sure all previous utilities have been paid for and canceled
- ☐ Follow up on changes of address for:
    - ☐ Banks
    - ☐ Credit cards
    - ☐ IRS
    - ☐ Loans
    - ☐ Insurance companies
    - ☐ Pension plans
    - ☐ Attorneys
    - ☐ Accountants
    - ☐ Physicians

- ☐ Newspapers
- ☐ Magazines
- ☐ Professional licenses
- ☐ Memberships
- ☐ Other

☐ If you didn't or weren't able to schedule advance appointments, make those appointments now to update your address for:
- ☐ Driver's license
- ☐ Vehicle registration
- ☐ Voter registration
- ☐ State and local tax forms

☐ Open any new bank accounts

☐ If you live in a condominium or subdivision with a homeowners association, figure out where to send your monthly dues and who to call for any maintenance issues and requests.

NOTE FROM ANDREW:
I believe this list is comprehensive.
But in the event that I've missed something,
I want to know. Please send an email
to **admin@andrewmellen.com**
so we can update this list,
and if I use your tip, I'll mention
you in the revised version.

Tips & Tricks

Trust me—there's a right way and a wrong way to move. I've learned that from experience. If you like to make things harder on yourself for no reason, carry on without a plan. But if you'd like to save time, money, and heartache by making smart decisions about your move *before* you begin, then read on.

CHECK THE CALENDAR

- Certain times of the year are busier moving times. Most people move between May and September when their kids are out of school. Busier means harder to book—and more expensive, since movers often charge peak pricing for popular times like weekends and summers.
- **To avoid peak pricing, schedule your move during off-peak times if you can.** The cheapest time of the year to move is between October and April, so if it's possible to postpone your move, do so. You may even be able to take advantage of special rates or promotions around holidays. Weekdays are typically cheaper than weekends, too.
- It is important to book your moving services well ahead to secure your ideal moving date.
- Remember that time is important on moving day. For instance, if you have a waterbed, it is likely to take around two hours to empty the water. So, plan ahead and consider doing certain tasks the night before.

AVOIDABLE MISTAKES

- When looking for properties, don't forget to measure the space for your refrigerator and other kitchen or laundry appliances.
- Find out if your homeowner's or renter's insurance policy covers your belongings in transit.
- Remember that all pools and spas that can hold water must have appropriate barriers to prevent access by young children.

- Compare measurements of the doorways and hallways in your new home to make sure your large and bulky items will fit. You may have to decide whether the new location or your things are more important and then sell or donate some items.
- Don't forget to be environmentally friendly! Flatten all your moving boxes for recycling. Many moving companies will pick them up after your move.

KNOW WHO TO TELL

Updating your address can be one of the most tedious parts of moving, so it's better to start early.

- Create a change of address log by writing down who you receive mail from each day. Then, contact those organizations with your change of address each morning or evening. This breaks up the task and helps make sure you aren't missing important contacts.
- Most important are banks, credit and store cards, Social Security, Medicare/Medicare, pension providers, insurance companies, loan providers, local tax authorities, employers, schools, your cable provider, and your doctor(s).
- At minimum, file a Temporary Change of Address with the U.S. Post Office to buy you time before you notify everyone else.
- Remember to organize switching off any phone lines, Internet connection and all your utilities, as well as arranging them to be connected at the other end.

DON'T FORGET THE BILLS AND EXPENSES

- It is important to arrange finances for quick cash to cover unexpected or emergency moving-related expenses.
- Make sure that direct debit and billing links to your bank accounts are organized to handle any changes resulting from your move.
- Be sure to settle all bills that may be overlooked in the move a few days before moving day.

- Budget wisely for forgotten items you may need once you move into your new home. Did you remember to find out if your home comes with a hose, for instance?
- Make sure to get several free moving quotes to help you better estimate the price of your move.

IF YOU DON'T NEED IT, DON'T MOVE IT

- Getting rid of clutter will simplify your life and lighten the load in the moving truck since movers base their prices on the volume of what you're shipping.
- 8 weeks before your move, tour your home and pull out everything you don't use or haven't used in the past 2 years. Exceptions may be sentimental objects, but pay attention to the story you're telling yourself about that ab-roller or treadmill. Sell it, donate it or give it away before you move. [See the following chapter for more guidelines on what not to take with you.]
- I've seen way too many clients toss everything into a box only to discard half of it when they unpack weeks later. Ouch.
- Things that you have a hard time parting with, but which will inevitably be stored in a garage, storage facility, or shed after the move should be packed in stackable containers that are rodent and dust proof.

TAKE CARE OF YOUR FOOD

- Be prepared to order take-out food or eat out on the first couple of nights in your new home. Chances are you'll feel too tired to cook, but even if you do feel like cooking, most of your kitchen appliances and tools will probably still be packed away.
- Make sure you use up your frozen foods or dispose of ones you have not used. Never let them thaw and try to refreeze them again. Not only will there be less to transport, but you will also avoid the risk of food spoilage.

DO RIGHT BY THE BUYERS

- It is important to make it quite clear to prospective buyers/tenants exactly what is included with the property. Are any appliances included? What about window treatments, rugs, etc.?
- You should always shut and lock all windows and doors as you leave your old home on moving day.

DEDUCT YOUR MOVING EXPENSES FROM YOUR TAXES

- Save every receipt—from gas to lodging to the move itself.
- If you relocated for a new full-time job at least 50 miles away from your previous home, you can deduct the cost of packing, transporting or storing your household goods from next year's tax return.
- For more information about tax-deductible moving expenses, check out the IRS Publication 521.

Getting Ready to Pack

Before you start shoving everything you own into boxes, you'll want to take a second to figure out your strategy. Not everything belongs on the moving truck, either because you shouldn't take it with you at all, or because it requires a bit of special planning.

THINGS *NOT* TO PACK
Anything that is hazardous, perishable, or unwanted should not be moved to your new home.

Hazardous Materials
Dispose of hazardous materials. Do not pack them up in boxes for movers to take to your new home. It is dangerous and illegal for movers to transport them. Give them away to neighbors or call your local waste management center, recycling company or the Environmental Protection Agency about how to safely dispose of them.

Hazardous materials include these flammable, corrosive and explosive items:

- Acid
- Aerosols
- Ammunition
- Batteries
- Car Batteries
- Charcoal
- Chemistry Sets
- Cleaning Fluid
- Fertilizer
- Fireworks
- Gasoline Poisons
- Kerosene
- Lamp Oil
- Lighter Fluid
- Liquid Bleach
- Loaded Weapons
- Matches
- Motor Oil
- Nail Polish & Remover
- Paints
- Paint Thinner
- Pesticides
- Propane Tanks
- Weed Killer

Perishable Items

Plants, food and animals are perishable items; they easily spoil, die or suffer damages if not specially cared for along the way. Many movers refuse to accept any kind of perishable items but may make an exception if the move is less than 150 miles and within a 24-hour drive away.

There may be restrictions, however, about moving perishable food or plants across a state line. A few agricultural states have strict rules about bringing plants and fruit into their state. Call your local U.S. Department of Agriculture to check on regulations before driving across state lines with perishable items.

Unwanted Items

The third category of things not to pack isn't as straightforward as the first two, and undertaking a big decluttering project right now might not appeal to you. But since you don't want to spend money, time and energy moving things you don't want, this is actually the perfect time to get yourself organized—and it's not as difficult as it sounds.

Before you even decide what stays and what can go, you need to sort Like With Like. It will be so much easier to make decisions about your stuff when all similar items are together. When things are isolated, story and sentimental attachment is harder to separate from the object itself. When you have 20 of the same kind of thing together, each individual item becomes less special unless it is really special.

Sorting Prayer

"Let me be careful and conscious, respectful and thoughtful.
Let me be deliberate and diligent and thorough.
Let me be strong and patient and flexible and resilient.
Let me be kind and generous and gracious and fearless.
And let this be pleasant."

HOW TO SORT
Supplies:
- Trash bags
- Egg timer or stopwatch
- Sorting tarps/blankets
- Dust cloths
- Acid free wrapping paper
- Non-invasive adhesives (tapes, glues)
- Tubs/containers/baskets to corral and contain like things
- Label-maker, or labels
- Fine-tip magic markers

Clear as large an area as you can manage. Then begin assembling "Like With Like" objects together until everything you're sorting has been matched with its siblings or left in 'one-off' piles of individual items.

GUIDE TO SORTING & MAKING DECISIONS

Refer to this section throughout the packing process—you'll also find these pages as a downloadable PDF in the Resources section.

Keep
Things you really love today, not only items that you loved many years ago, and items you feel confident you'll continue to love in many years to come. If destined for storage, these will be wrapped in acid-free paper or other protective coverings (as needed) and placed in containers for safekeeping.

Return to others before you move
Things that belong to other people which are currently in your possession. It doesn't matter how long you've had them, they need to go home and sooner rather than later. Do not procrastinate any longer, swallow whatever feelings you may have about the amount of time you've had them, and get them gone.

In these cases you may give away the object RATHER than returning them to their owner:
- The owner is deceased and you are unable (not unwilling) to contact next of kin;
- The return of the object would cause harm to the recipient

  or someone other than yourself.

Give away before you move
Things you are clearly done with that you're now willing to give away. For mementos, it's uncertain how many of these kinds of things have a life beyond you. For any that still have utility, determine where they would best be further used and send them there. Do not waste time searching for the 'perfect' home.

Where to donate:
- Thrift store/shelter
- Specific people/ organizations
- Freecycle/Craigslist/Curb with a sign

Sell (only things that have significant value and easy-to-identify markets)
Things you are clearly done with that have adequate value to demand a sale. Taken to a local consignment shop or sold online, either by yourself or through a drop-off service that manages online auctions for you.

Trash
The unfortunate things you've kept which have no value to anyone and are to now be discarded.

The fence
As in, "to be on the fence," or unable to make a decision. This is not a mask for procrastination or regret, but only for cases of true confoundment.

NOT A "GET OUT OF JAIL FREE" CARD — use only as a last resort.

If you find yourself saying "but…" a lot during this process, remember that anything you're able to get rid of now is one less item that you'll have to pay to relocate AND deal with during and after the move.

BUT....IT WAS A GIFT!
Nothing freely given is ever meant to be a burden. This is the fundamental concept behind giving and receiving gifts. Most gifts are being offered in a spirit of kindness and thoughtfulness, and a desire to enhance your quality of life—not to saddle you with an unnecessary object. If a gifted item isn't aesthetically pleasing or practical to you, feel free to get rid of it. The act of giving—rather than the object itself—is the gift.

...I CAN'T GET RID OF PHOTOS OF _____!
Sure you can, and should. Only keep photos that inspire an immediate emotional response in you—if it's just a picture, let it go. Ask yourself the following questions about each photo, and discard it if the answer is no:

- Is the print properly exposed?
- Is the subject in focus?
- Is the subject completely in the frame?
- Is the subject obscured by anything (thumbs, straps, signs, etc)?
- Is the photo flattering?
- Is the photo of an event or person you'd like to remember?
- Do you know everyone, or anyone, in the photo?
- Do you care about everyone, or anyone, in the photo? (Really think about pictures of exes)
- Will you ever want reprints of this image? Would anyone else?
- If it's a close duplicate of other shots, is it superior?

If you answered "yes," the photo is a keeper. Record identifying description on the back of these photos, such as date taken, key subjects, or people in the photo. Separate out favorite pics to display as you come across them and segregate any pics that are earmarked for family or friends (such as duplicates).

If you plan to store your photos in boxes, sort directly into those boxes (no need to touch them twice). Albums or scrapbooks require more planning in terms of theme and layout—be honest with yourself about whether this is a good time to take on such a project.

If you've been considering digitizing print photographs, now may be the time. You can ship them off to a service and the digital images will be shipped back to you at your new address.

...I MIGHT NEED IT [OR FINALLY READ IT] SOMEDAY!
Financial/banking documents
Hang onto statements/canceled checks from the past seven years, but you can likely get rid of monthly/quarterly statements where year-end statement reflects 12 months' transactions and unused checks for closed accounts. Confirm with your accountant if you're reluctant to dispose of these.

Receipts
There are only 8 kinds of receipts that you need to keep:
1. Capital improvements to a piece of real estate you own
2. Major purchases, such as appliances
3. Services and repairs to either your home or vehicle
4. Tax-deductible expenses
5. Reimbursable expenses
6. Medical expenses where documentation is needed
7. Cash receipts
8. Items you are not yet committed to keeping and may return to the store

If you have receipts outside of these categories, shred and dispose of them now. Deal with any #8 items prior to moving.

Periodicals, catalogs, and articles
Periodicals older than 3 months should be discarded. If you haven't read it within this time frame, it is unlikely that you'll read it now—especially after you've moved.

A note on articles or recipes clipped out of periodicals: If you've ever uttered the words, "I just don't have enough time," then be very clear with yourself about the choices you're making when you choose to hold onto something torn out of a periodical unless you're a librarian by trade. If you don't have a specific plan for the information in your hands, let it go or scan it, label it properly, and THEN let it go. There is no reason to save the printed version.

Miscellaneous documents
Hang onto owner's manuals and installation instructions for items that will be moving with you to your new home. A quick online search may yield digital (PDF) versions of these manuals and instructions, in which case you may choose to download and save them and recycle the paper versions.

You don't need to keep manuals for items you aren't keeping, or expired warranties and service contracts (though you may wish to harvest key support contact information first to add to your address/phone book).

In terms of papers and documents, consider this:
80% of the information we keep, we never use.

You don't need to keep any of the following:
- Duplicates of anything (Unless copied specifically for someone else—in which case, create an envelope, address it, and mail it now)
- Schedules/itineraries that are complete or outdated (Keep calendars or other documentation of where you were and when, if trips were a business expense or you like keeping track of your travels)
- Generic account info/privacy statements you've read or don't intend to read
- Expired insurance policies (Compare new to old first—is coverage consistent and accurate?)
- Business cards from anyone whose name you don't recognize
- Maps/atlases that are more than three years old
- Brochures from tourist destinations (Whether you've been there or not, these are not souvenirs)

Mail

Don't pack unopened mail! Even if—especially if—you have a large backlog of old mail, you'll want to deal with it before you move. Refer to the Resources chapter for a step-by-step guide to going through old mail.

Now that you've got everything sorted out, let's talk about special items that won't get packed in boxes.

Irreplaceable Items

There are some items that you won't want to pack up with the rest of your belongings. Things of importance and information you need on hand should be carried with you during your move, not transported by movers. Some of these may not have much monetary value, but they could be very difficult or impossible to replace.

- Address Books
- Airline Tickets
- Bonds
- Cameras
- Car Keys
- Check Books
- Computer Disks
- Computer Software
- Confidential Client Files (If you're a doctor, lawyer or therapist)
- Diaries
- Deeds
- Financial Records
- Jewelry
- Loose Photos and Photo Albums
- Medical Records
- Personal Files
- Personal Letters
- Prescription Medicines
- Research Projects

Extraordinary Value Items

Anything worth more than $100 a pound is considered an Extraordinary Value Item. If you decide to have your movers move your extraordinary value items, you need to make an inventory list identifying each one and then advise your mover in writing of their existence before the move. Most van lines have a special High Value Inventory Form for you to fill out for this purpose so that items can be properly accounted for at the point of origin and noted as being delivered in good condition at the conclusion of the move. Movers' insurance policies will likely not adequately cover the value of these items if they're not properly documented in advance. Extraordinary Value items include:

- Antiques
- Art Collections
- Audio Equipment
- Cameras
- Coin Collections
- Computers
- Computer Software
- Currency
- Figurines
- Flat panel TVs
- Furs
- Jewelry
- Musical Instruments, including pianos
- Oriental Rugs
- Precious Stones/Gems
- Printers
- Silver & Silverware

Depending on the nature of your valuables, you may wish to arrange for a specialty mover to handle these. For example, valuables like fine art and pianos are often moved by companies that specialize in the specific challenges of handling these kinds of items.

Working with Professional Movers

PLANNING THE MOVE

Hazardous Materials
If you're hiring a professional moving company, do your research. To make sure you're getting the best price possible, get at least three estimates. Be wary of companies that won't give you an estimate up front—you're almost guaranteed an unpleasant surprise from them on the back end.

Compare Apples to Apples
All moving companies are not the same. Some companies offer flat rates while others bid low but then pile on the additional charges when it's time to settle the bill, so be careful when comparing the bottom line. To get an accurate estimate of your total, you'll want to find out about "extras" such as flights of stairs, packing materials and parking tickets. If a rate sounds too good to be true, it probably is.

Insurance
Since you are trusting someone else with your possessions, make sure you're covered in case anything is lost or damaged. Don't wait until the day of the big move to figure out insurance since you will have enough to think about.

Moving companies are required by federal law to offer two types of liability coverage for interstate moves (and many offer the same for local moves too):

Released value, which is free to you but offers minimal protection: under this option, the mover assumes liability for up to 60 cents per pound per article, which does not cover the value of most household items. (For example: If your 30-pound LCD flat-screen television was destroyed, you'd be reimbursed $18 for it.) This simply isn't practical, so you'll want to obtain additional coverage.

Full value is a more comprehensive plan, available to you at an additional cost. The mover is liable for the replacement value of your items. If any of your personal property is lost, destroyed or damaged while in your mover's custody, your mover will, at its discretion, offer to:

- Repair
- Replace
- Make a cash settlement for the cost of the repair or the current market replacement value.

The cost for Full Value Protection liability coverage varies by moving company and by the deductible level you select. You may pay more for better coverage, but remember: there's no price tag on your own peace of mind.

Moving companies may only accept liability for items that were packed by their staff. Items packed by the owner are not covered in many cases, unless specifically mentioned in the moving agreement.

Note that for Extraordinary Value items (anything worth more than $100 per pound), you will need to complete a High Value Inventory List from your moving company, regardless of the level of insurance coverage you select. Full value coverage will not apply to Extraordinary Value items that were not itemized on the inventory list.

You can also protect yourself with third party insurance coverage—insurance offered by an insurance company, rather than by the moving company. Spend the money for real insurance and make sure you buy it from a reputable carrier that has an excellent record for paying out damages. The last thing you want to do after moving is to spend 6 months fighting for them to pay a claim. Check your homeowner's or renter's insurance policy as well—many will cover approximately 10 percent of the value of your personal property.

When making your choice regarding insurance, it is worth comparing the ease of filing a claim through the moving company's liability coverage versus your own insurance. An hour or two of research here will be invaluable should you need to file a claim later. If the insurance company provided by the mover has a lousy history of paying claims, get your own insurance. You'll be upset enough if something is damaged—it serves you to make filing a claim easy and not an additional source of stress. No one expects damage. Do not let your natural optimism or procrastination undermine being adequately covered and prepared for the worst.

Don't be seduced by random movers

Even if you're not especially attached to your possessions, you're still moving them, right? So don't hand your precious things over to "two men and a van" on Craigslist without checking the BBB and at least 3 references. There are bargains, and then there are hustlers. If you can't tell the difference, you're probably better off going with an established moving company or loyal friends.

Use your own packing supplies
Moving companies mark up packing supplies—regardless of what they tell you. You can save money by using any containers and materials you already have on hand, including laundry baskets and trash bags. Use towels and other linens to wrap items and for padding. You can buy any additional packing from a source like Uline.com or a recycled box company—or get them free from a local business like a grocery or liquor store.

MOVING DAY ETIQUETTE

Be ready
Unless you opt for a Full Service move, meaning the moving company will pack your possessions for you, it's a good idea to be completely finished packing by the time the movers arrive. You're paying for their time—so you won't want them to spend it waiting for you to finish packing up your boxes.

Labels matter
If a box contains something fragile, make sure it's clearly marked on the outside, on the top of each carton and on at least one side. Up arrows indicating which way you want boxes moved helps for things that shouldn't be put on their sides. Labeling each container with its destination in your new home will also make the movers' jobs easier and will save time (especially important if you're being charged by the hour). You can create a color coded chart for each room or simply call out each room/location on each container.

Accessibility is everything
This applies both to you and to your old and new homes.

Make sure you are accessible to the movers for the entire duration in case they have questions or concerns. Any delays caused by your absence may affect price as well as timing.

It's also important to determine in advance where they can park. Are there any parking restrictions? Do you need any special permits for the street? What about the impact on neighbors and their commutes? Consider egress when planning for larger vehicles and anticipating how long they will be parked.

If there are multiple entrances, you should identify in advance which doors everyone should use.

Tipping

Moving is a service industry, and consensus has it that 5% of the move cost (equally divided between all movers) or $20 per mover is standard. If you received exceptional service, you can reward that service with a larger tip. If the service was not good, you should not feel obligated to tip and you should never be forced to tip. You should always hand the tip to each mover—never give a lump sum to the foreman or one mover and ask them to distribute it for you, for obvious reasons.

DIY Packing & Moving

Moving yourself is the cheapest way to go, financially. You'll definitely save money handling the process on your own. It's helpful to consider all the costs of packing, loading and possibly driving cross-country. In addition to the impact on your wallet, there's also the impact on your body. And if you are not good at project managing, DIY moving can be a frustrating process. Forewarned is forearmed, so consider carefully what you are saving versus what you are spending when you choose this option.

PACKING SUPPLIES
Use what you have, and then buy your own supplies
Save money by filling up containers you already have, like suitcases or plastic bins. Use sheets and linens to wrap items. Buy the packing materials you still need from a recycled box company, or get them free from a local business—grocery stores and liquor stores still give away cartons.

You'll want the following supplies handy:
- Boxes
- Marking pen
- Bubble wrap
- Unprinted newspaper and tissue
- Tape and scissors
- Tape measure
- Boxes designed for breakables or special items, such as dishes or wardrobe

HOW TO PACK BOXES

Select the proper size and type of carton for the job
Heavy items such as books, record albums, canned food, etc. should be put in smaller cartons. Ensure that each carton is not too heavy for one person to easily move it. You're better off moving a few more boxes than throwing out your back.

Items such as large pictures, mirrors, glass tops and shelves, clocks, TVs and mattresses will require special cartons.

Pack audio-video equipment and computers in their original

boxes, if you have them. If you don't, use heavy-duty cartons to protect them in transit.

Label all cables and tighten transit screws when you are disconnecting equipment. This will make reassembling things in your new home quick and easy. If you remove any screws or other fasteners, tape them to the objects they are removed from.

Back up your software and data files to an external drive. These drives should be moved with your personal papers.

Insert cardboard or an old disk into disk drives.

Unhook all cables and power cords, labeling their positions for ease in set up. Pack cords with any manuals and software disks.

Use only static-free packing materials such as clean-wadded unprinted newsprint. Do NOT use bubble wrap or peanuts around electronics.

Use wadded paper on bottom of carton. Also use wadded paper to fill in around the item.

Remove all ink and toner cartridges from printers and copiers before packing.

Pack liquid medicines in a leak-proof container, but remember to keep any medications you or a member of your household are currently taking with you during the move rather than packing in boxes.

Tape the bottom of cartons
Taping the bottom of cartons before filling them prevents the cartons from accidentally opening up in transit and having your contents spill out the bottom during the move. Best practice is five pieces of tape for each bottom. One goes across the center seam with two others spaced equally across the bottom, then tape each corner edge where there is a seam.

Heavy items on the bottom/light items on the top
In each container the heavier items should be placed at the bottom and the lighter items on top to prevent damage.

Use a lot of paper
All breakable items should be wrapped individually in paper. Paper should be used to cushion the bottom, sides and top of every carton.

Place breakables correctly in carton
Plates should be stacked vertically as if in a dish drain; glasses and stemware should be placed in an upright position; again, use plenty of paper on all fragile and breakable items.

Correctly fill cartons
Fill all cartons to the top without overfilling. Cartons with items sticking up beyond the top can't be properly closed or stacked; underfilled cartons tend to crush when stacked.

A small space at the top can be filled with paper, a towel, a blanket or other similar items—that's the simplest way to completely fill a carton rather than forcing a hard-edged item into the carton to fill any small open spaces.

Best practice is to keep all cartons below 50 pounds — if you can't easily guesstimate what 50 pounds feels like, remember that the goal is to have every carton light enough that one person can lift it and move it by themselves.

Close carton and seal with tape
Cartons should be closed-top and sealed with tape to prevent damage and make stacking easier.

Label each carton
Use a marker to clearly label each carton. The label should describe the general contents AND the room it is to be placed in at destination.

You can label the top of the carton—you should also label at least one side of each carton so that stacked cartons can be identified.

If you need a carton to always remain upright, draw arrows on each side indicating which end must always be kept up. Any cartons containing fragile items should be labeled as such.

In addition to labeling with words, you can use different colored stickers or index cards for each box. Then at your new home, you can place a sticker or index card of the corresponding color on the trim or door frame outside the room to make matching colors easy for you and your crew.

For the tech-savvy mover, you can create a spreadsheet to itemize all your belongings or use an app to track items. Just be mindful of complicating your move and getting lost in a digital haze when the goal is simply getting everything you own from one place to another intact.

Stacking cartons
You'll save time on your move if you use dollies or a hand truck. If you use dollies, you can load them four feet high and still move them easily. For hand trucks, stack similarly sized cartons no more than five feet high. Then slide the hand truck's blade under the stack to roll the cartons from your home to the truck.

Packing everyday essentials
Pack a carton of items you will need immediately at the destination and set these aside to load last so this will be the first carton you unload. Label it "unpack first" or "essentials" to avoid confusion.
Items you may need include:
- Screwdrivers, flat head and Phillips
- Hammer
- Toilet paper
- Hand and dish soap
- Toothpaste and brushes
- Towels
- Paper towels
- Kettle, coffee maker and tea/coffee
- Paper plates and cups
- Eating and cooking utensils

PACKING FURNITURE

Furniture should be wrapped with packing blankets or heavy-duty paper wrap. There are environmental concerns with both tape and shrink wrap—you can read more about them both here and then decide which you'll use to secure packing: https://sustainablepackaging.org/

Finials and other decorative items that are easily removed from furniture should be put in a ziplock or other bag, labeled and placed in a drawer or cabinet in the piece of furniture or taped to the piece of furniture they belong to.

Any fasteners used to hold furniture together should also be gathered into a ziplock or other bag, properly labeled and attached to its furniture piece.

Local Moves
For local moves, you can get away with not wrapping mattresses and box springs, bed frames and other large and bulky items. If you don't want to individually pack mirrors, large pictures and other items containing glass, you should at least lightly wrap them and stack them vertically inside a commercial bin (called a C-bin for short in the moving trade). C-bins are also helpful to corral odd-shaped and random items that didn't get packed individually, such as vacuum cleaners, throw rugs and step stools. Lamps and lampshades should always be individually packed.

RENT A TRUCK, VAN OR TRAILER

You can rent a truck, van or trailer and get your friends and family to pitch in packing, loading and unloading—just be prepared to return the favor or at least buy a meal or two.

When renting a truck or van, research the rental company's as well as your credit card's damage policy. Most rental companies offer multiple levels of damage coverage—you should compare this with what your credit card company also offers.

If you opt out of damage coverage from the rental company and your credit card company does NOT provide coverage, you'll be liable for the full cost of the damage—regardless of fault. If you own a car, check your car's insurance policy as well to see if it covers you while driving a rented vehicle.

If you're using a trailer, make sure your vehicle can easily tow the full weight of the loaded trailer. Some trailer rental companies will install a receiver and hitch for you if you don't already have one. If not, most mechanics can do this for you—just make sure the receiver, hitch and ball match the load of the trailer. Like trucks, hitches come in multiple classes.

For any rental, make sure to read the fine print for rental duration, mileage allowances and fuel surcharges, in case you were planning to combine a vacation with your cross-country move.

CONSIDER PORTABLE STORAGE AND DELIVERY

Companies like PODS, 1-800-PACKRAT, MAKE SPACE and BOXIE 24 will deliver a storage unit or reusable tubs to your door. You pack them yourself, and then the company picks up and delivers the containers to any address within their territory. This saves you the stress and hassle of driving your stuff yourself, and is considerably less expensive than using professional movers to pack and transport your stuff.

Children & Moving

Before leaving your old home behind, it's important to help your children prepare for this transition. They may be fine with moving or they may need some support and guidance in saying goodbye to their home.

TIPS FOR MOVING WITH KIDS

Involve your child in the moving process

Moving is difficult for everyone. Your relocation will go much more smoothly if your kids are kept in the loop about the details. After all, you are making the arrangements so you are all too familiar with the daily ups and downs. Include them and they will be, too. And you'll also be teaching them some life skills in the process.

Write your moving date on the family calendar and keep reminding everyone in the house of any upcoming deadlines. It's a good idea to also write the date you'll start packing.

Allow young children to pack their favorite toys and other non-essential items. This gives them a sense of participation. It's less important that the boxes be perfectly packed—it's more important that they feel integrated into the process.

Older children can be tasked with packing up their rooms and household items. You can give them markers, crayons, stickers and labels so they can decorate their boxes, if they like art projects. If you have more than one child, make sure they each get distinct colors and stickers so mapping the cartons to their new rooms is easier.

You could also give your children a floor plan of their new room(s) so they can plan ahead for where furniture and toys will be placed once you get there.

Fun music will create a positive mood when it's time to start packing and unpacking. The TV may be too distracting so packing it early will eliminate any temptation to turn it on.

Help your kids get familiar with their new surroundings

If it makes sense and you can afford it, take your children to your new home or town in advance of the move so they can look around and become familiar with the location. If the timing doesn't work or it's cost-prohibitive, take pictures or videos on one of your trips there to share with them when you get home. This will help them recognize various landmarks when you arrive.

Help them get involved in their new school and community
Making friends and doing activities they enjoy will help ease the transition for your child, so do a little research in advance to jump start the process for them. Check out your new neighborhood for sports, dance, art and other programs your kids enjoy, along with theaters, libraries and community centers.

For music, dance and art lessons, make sure you find a new teacher in your new location so there is as little disruption as possible.

If you sense your child is particularly upset about the move, you can alert teachers, coaches and caregivers so they can help with the transition on their end.

Have a going-away party
There's no avoiding both the bitter and the sweet of a move so hosting a going-away party is a great way to confront the beast head on.

You can ask party guests to write special notes for your child in a notebook or to prepare a few cards they can open in the new home to provide something novel and familiar as they get acclimated. Signing a T-shirt or stuffed animal is another way to bring their old friends with them.

Definitely have an address book at the party where friends can write down their contact information, including email and social media accounts. A stack of fun, self-addressed postcards to your child is another way to ensure their friends from home will stay in touch for some time.

Continue family traditions
Stick to your established family routines and schedules, even as your physical environment is shifting. If Wednesday is always pizza night, don't change it. Any lessons, groups or events they participate in should continue right up until you leave. The more stable and routine you keep your current home and make your new home, the less disruptive the move will be for your child.

Keep it positive

Even if you're not thrilled about the move, everyone is looking to you to inform how they should feel about the move. If you're whiny and complaining, you should not be surprised to find that behavior mirrored by your children. Likewise, if you're upbeat without being fake or obnoxious, they too will find ways to stay positive about the situation.

Your attitude sets the tone for the household. The better you are at adapting and adjusting, the better of an example you'll be setting for your kids. Remember, the move is an event and it's also an opportunity for teaching your child how to meet unexpected circumstances and change. That lesson is invaluable as they mature. Take advantage of this moment to instruct them in the best ways to face the unexpected so they are prepared as possible in the future to meet adventures, adversity and tragedy as an adult.

Pets & Moving

Moving is a big deal for everyone involved, including your pets—maybe even more so for them, since they don't understand what's happening. Here are some ways you can ease the stress on your furry friends.

BEFORE THE MOVE

Assemble a few days' worth of food, litter, and toys so you can make your pet comfortable while you unpack.

If you're moving to a another city, contact your vet so you can take medical records and prescriptions with you. Ask for a vet recommendation near your new home.

If you'll be moving a long distance and flying to a new home, consider arranging a ground transport pet shipping service for your pet. While you can fly with some types of pets, animals that are placed in the cargo area of a plane are considered "luggage," and treated accordingly. The cargo area is not climate-controlled and experiences extreme temperatures and oxygen levels. A pet shipper will be with your pet at all times in a comfortable environment.

DURING THE MOVE

Consider arranging for a kennel or a friend to keep your pet on moving day, but if that's not possible, secure your pet in the quietest part of the house or in a carrier in your vehicle (provided the space is a safe temperature). Provide food and water, and check on them regularly.

Take the pet to your new house in your own vehicle, not the moving truck.

Set up as much as you can before you introduce your pet to the new house.

AFTER THE MOVE

Confine your pet to one section of the house while they adjust to being in a new space. Food, water, litter box, toys, and pet beds should all be located here temporarily. When they seem to be comfortable, gradually introduce them to other rooms.

You can move food and litter boxes to their permanent home gradually too, if necessary.

If your pet is microchipped, be sure to update the address on file.

Give your pet lots of attention and affection!

Moving with Disabilities

If you or someone in your family has a disability—whether visible or invisible—some aspects of moving may require additional preparation or time both on your part and on the part of your moving company.

COMMUNITY RESOURCES

Organizations such as the Independent Living Research Utlilization and Centers for Independent Living offer resources throughout the US. Projects at the University of New Hampshire and ICDRI maintain robust websites of online publications and other resources. You'll find additional resources at the US Department of Labor's Office of Disability Employment site.

BENEFITS

If you are moving to another state, check to see if your disability benefits will be affected. You can visit the Social Security Administration for more information.

Likewise, look into any available moving assistance that either your new or old city of residence may offer.

FINANCIAL AID

Organizations such as National Institute on Life Planning for People with Disabilities, ADAPT, and AUCD may offer financial assistance to help defray the costs of your move. To reduce monthly utility bills, check out Operation Roundup.

ACCESSIBILITY

Perform an assessment ahead of time so you can make any adjustments prior to moving in. From the front door to the garage, check to see how easily doors open, how high the counters, sinks, fixtures and switches are, how wide the hallways and doorways are, and if you need any ramps or other devices installed. If you are renting, modifications and accommodations should be discussed with your future landlord before signing any leases. Keep an eye out for hazards on the floor like cords, cables and doorstops.

HIRE AN EXPERIENCED MOVER

Consider hiring a moving company who has relocated people with disabilities before. Ask for references from people with disabilities who've used the service in the past.

OPT FOR A FULL-SERVICE MOVE

This may make the process easier, since the moving company will pack and unpack your belongings for you.

FIND HEALTH CARE SERVICES NEARBY

Research the nearest emergency care facilities, then add them to your phone and share them with your family and friends. Likewise, find the closest pharmacy, refill your prescriptions before you move, and forward the pharmacy's contact information to all your doctors.

Resources

This guide is here to help you plan, sort, and tackle every last object in your home and item on your moving to-do list. Throughout the book, I mention additional resouces that you can use to organize your belongings once and for all. Now it's time to turn you loose with those resources!

To download the supplemental materials mentioned throughout this book, visit

www.andrewmellen.com/moving

Downloadable resources include:

⤓ Printable Ultimate Moving Checklist

⤓ Current Size List

⤓ Sorting Old Mail

⤓ How to File Papers

⤓ Should It Stay or Should It Go?

⤓ Global Categories for Stuff

Need to do more than just pack and move? We've got lots of ways to help you get and stay organized for good.

You can read (or listen to) my best-selling book *Unstuff Your Life!*

The Unstuff Your Life System Workbook is a great companion to *Unstuff Your Life!*

And if you're looking for a total life transformation, you need *The Unstuff Your Life System*™. It's a simple yet comprehensive 7-Step program that walks you step-by-step and week-by-week from clutter and chaos to a calm, organized and efficient workplace, home, car, and other spaces. For good.

For more information on
Unstuff Your Life!
visit **http://bit.ly/unstuffmellen**

For more information on
The Unstuff Your Life System™
visit **www.andrewmellen.com/uyls**

Made in the USA
Las Vegas, NV
22 October 2021